THE FEATHER

Poems by
Ann Murray

Title: *The Feather, Poems by Ann Murray*
Author: *Ann Murray*
Category: *Poetry*

Self-published via Amazon Blurb, 2015
© Ann Murray

Other publications from the author:

The Blueness Above
Travelling Light
Heaven's Bright Stall
The Beautiful Gate
Washed by the Light of the Stars

Visit the author's blog at:

www.asmorningrising.blogspot.co.uk

"The greatest challenge of the day is:
how to bring about a revolution of the heart,
a revolution which has to start with each one of us?"

- Dorothy Day

Acknowledgements

I would like to thank my brother John McKeever who has faithfully stood by me in editing this book as well as the previous books, and also sincere thanks to my son Declan Murray whose talents and attention to detail have been to the fore in this publication.

Contents

The Feather

A magpie feather on the lawn
Is a quill dipped into the inkwell of the earth.
Sooner or later a sympathetic breeze
Will liberate it from its hold.
The open heart can decipher
These traces of scripted Ogham*, barely visible on the grass.

Nature surely has something interesting to say
When she stops us in our tracks
Choosing as muse
A feather delighting her heart.

* Early Medieval alphabet used primarily to write the early
Irish language.

Instrument of Your Plan

Allow Lord that I may be shaped by the holy silence
Of night skies
Moulded by my creator's hand
So as to be material for your purpose
Instrument of your plan.

Allow Lord that I will be docile to your will
That I will bend like grass in the wind
Move as one spirited
And animated by the breath of your love.

Gaze of the Divine

Month after month it seemed the earth held all the
promise of an empty purse. Suddenly then, a single
pale and slender stalk was proof of hidden works,
of tenacity thrust towards the sun, of soul search
and mad abundance! What can it be but glory, for
glory sings its own unique song. It dances on the
green when we are blessed, when the sun-seeking
eye meets the gaze of the divine, forever fixed on
all that he has made.

Oceans of Light

In sudden isolation
An odd scattering begins to sing.
The wren's cocked tail
Is like the rudder of his soul
Keeping the spirit afloat
On waves of light.

28th February 2015

Sometimes I am fed by waves and smiles
By crumbs of conversation
When my ear picks up words that
Sing of the joy of life.

Sometimes I am fed by gestures
When one person helps another
Or kisses a forehead as lined and furrowed
As an over-worked field.

Sometimes I am fed by silence
Sacred and mysterious
That romances my soul
And strikes in the cavern of my heart
A chord so rich that it makes me tremble.

And I realise
As if waking from a dream
That that which means most to me
Is forever present;
And it is only ever me
Who walks away.

To pray the rosary is to enter the enclosure of peace. Iconic images grace the walls and help us to contemplate the life of Jesus through various mysteries – joyful, sorrowful, luminous and glorious. Something transcendent and powerful draws us to the sacred place of prayer when the Angelus bell rings, reminding us of that moment in time when a young girl was visited by an angel and her life changed forever. Our lives too can change when we are open to the grace of God working in and through us.

–

We fall into habits accidentally rather than by consciously choosing them. Now before I leave the house I check my coat pocket for rosary beads. I pray when I'm walking along the city streets, and every so often I will touch the beads or pat my pocket with my fingertips just to make the contact physical as well as spiritual. In prayer we transcend the reality of the now that we find ourselves in.There is a coming down as well as a lifting up and somewhere in the middle of all that is us, and the intimacy we foster with God and through God, with Mary and through Mary; from our concrete streets to the heights of heaven.

Above All That Mars

Nothing holy will harm us
Or darken the spaces we clamber in
Nothing holy will snuff out the flame of faith
Unless to build a living fire
In the temple within.

Nothing holy will stain or taint
For holiness is good
As God is good.

We are like sparks flying
Across pewter smitten skies
Catching the eyes of those who seek answers,
Who yearn for simplicity and purpose
Above all that mars.

The simple light of faith that was at work in our fore-bearers was enough to drive them on. Satisfied to work with little reward, to rest with little comfort, and to go out to a secret place, and risk life and limb, to hear the word of God. What drove them is the same power that drives us; if our hearts are open, if our ears are open, we too can be Eucharistic people.

-

We must allow time for the journeying of the spoken word from one soul to another. Our willingness to listen is enhanced by our ability to remain silent in the sacred space of friendship.

-

Silence is the room we make for God. It has no walls; neither ceiling nor floor. It is a space we create within ourselves that houses Him, and thoughts of Him, and more.

The Saintly Trees

The deep purple sky
Is dusted with silver.
Trees etch their storm-cast statures
In black relief
And bow in homage to the latent poetry
Of the spaces they occupy.

The floral chorus of the forest rings out
As we gather and disperse.
The trees are always there
They are the giant ones of prayer.

Reconciliation

A cascade of tamarisk sways in the easterly breeze,
A blackbird sings a song of praise before first light
A blazing star on the charcoal coat of night
Is guide for the sea-farer cast on a troubled tide
Absolution is a hand raised high
Drawing down that which the world cannot give
And there is peace in the soul.

Saints of Ireland

We owe much to St Patrick, the giant one of prayer.
A hundred times he prayed, by day and night,
letting the flame of God's love melt away the
bitterness and resentment that was stifling his heart.
Who am I, if not a recipient of faith passed down?
What am I, if not a daughter of Erin? Where am I,
if not on a pilgrim path where the light of the saints
is a lamp to my feet? Saints of Ireland, pray for us,
whoever and wherever we may be, guide us by the
Word and by the hand, and lead us home.

Lullaby of Love

Like dappled light through the forest canopy God
finds a way to penetrate the darkness of life below.
We are drawn to him like we are drawn to stars in
a night sky. We never tire of this manifestation of
the infinitesimal power of God and the beauty of
creation, seeming to sing for us its own sweet
lullaby of love.

Easter Glory

Run to Him and love Him
Who was sorrowful onto death
See now his glory rise
As hearts take hold
And close within themselves the prize
The conquerer of death
No more despised.

Throw yourself at His feet and
Love Him because He loved us first
And refuse those dreams
That shut Him out!

Build your hope on the rolled-back stone
Of the Easter dawn
The victory won by the Risen Christ
For us, the sleeping dead,
And all the not-yet-born.

Easter

Easter brings many biblical characters to life in the story of the Passion. Their stories speak to us of both loyalty and betrayal. We meet Joseph of Aramithea and Our Lady of Sorrows and we are reminded of Simeon's prophecy. The two-fold cock crow echoes through the centuries and we are reminded of the weakness of humanity, the denial of light in the darkness of sin. When the dreaded hour comes we will be torn as the temple veil was torn, our souls rent by awe and passion. Hidden among the burial cloths we will glimpse the pulsing beauty of the stars.

Going Round in Circles

The beads are round
The prayer goes round
We contemplate the mysteries
Until we finish back where we started.

The beads dimple our fingertips
We kiss the cross with our lips
The prayer is said or sung
Nothing is unheard
Neither the Pater Noster
Nor the Ave
Nor the Gloria.

The beads are round
The prayer goes round
We find ourselves
Back where we started
Yet by holy design
We find we are in a new place
With Mary, through Mary,
Journeying to God.

Divine Mercy

Mercy is the breath of the living God
Entering the streets of our distress,
Bringing new hope where hope has been lost
Washing away all that burdens us
Even to the point of death.

Divine Mercy is a song-burst from the tree
Awakening in our drowsy souls
A desire to grow
When touched by grace and the power of God.

Mercy is a tree whose Calvary roots
Reach across the world
Whose worth is told in Babel tongues that praise
The Master, him of the pierced side,
Who by water and his blood
Saves the sinner from himself.

Window of His Eyes

He looks upon the world through the window of
His eyes
We are more beautiful than stars to him
In our breathing out and in
There is the movement of a thousand wings
And in the silent language of the soul
Light plays with light in facets fit for kings.
We have the treasures of the world and more
If we but trim our lamps
And gaze on Him.

Dancing Shoes

I saw
Dangling from a brooding tree
By the river's edge
A pair of dancing shoes.

At once I knew to whom
They belonged.
Only the lord of the dance
Could catch the eye of the beholder
With such artistry of light slung
On branches dark as night.

The Great Ones

We are the great ones
Feeding the hungry
Clothing the naked
Showering them with the
Leftovers of our bounty!

But wait....wait....
What is there to be complacent about?
We know in our hearts that the lives of children
Across the world
Are balanced between life and death.

Until that day comes
When we can stand
And look the world in the eye
Knowing that none go hungry
That all walk free
Wrapped in robes
Spun from the silken threads of justice....

Until that day comes
We would do better to imagine ourselves
As feathers on the weigh scale of eternity
Tilted, on an axis of prayer.

Mary of Graces

Mary of the mind - one with whom to share cares and aspirations.
Mary of the heart - the woman of sorrows who pondered many things in her heart.
Mary of the soul - the prayerful one of the Magnificat, the God-bearer, the Spouse of the Spirit, daughter of the Father, Mother of the Saviour of the world.
Mary of the hills – one who journeyed long to visit her cousin Elizabeth.
Mary of the sea – the star that shines most bright, the refuge from the storm.
Mary of the wilderness – our protectress and mantle.
Mary of the garden – the mystical rose whose fragrance enhances the world.
Mary of hope and joy – the woman of now, the hand that leads us away from what is done, and onwards to what is to come.
Mary of graces – blessed among women, there at the last.

Star of the Sea

I have read accounts of visionaries of Mary who spoke of the beauty of the Blessed Virgin as a beauty that left them speechless and rooted to the spot. The world's artists have created breathtakingly beautiful images of Mary but the visionaries tell us hers is a beauty that cannot be truly captured on canvas. We have neither eyes nor mind that can adequately take in the loveliness of the Mother of God. One born without sin, one conceived immaculately, with neither taint nor stain, and seated now as Queen of Heaven, must bear a unique type of beauty. Yet she is not distanced from us, she lived and worked among us and knows of the trials of life. She gazes upon us with motherly eyes. She shines like the sun, as light in our darkness. When we refer to Mary as Star of the Sea we are praying, pleading for refuge, for guidance, for a safe voyage across the world's seas. We implore the one who will take us at the hour of our death to heaven's gates and the merciful embrace of the Trinity.

-

To sing of Mary is not to praise God less. For through his mother's heart the world is blessed. All her graces are gifts from God, straight from the heart of heaven.

Our House

There were creaky stairs and drafty rooms and the
Net curtains sagged like limp flags.
The lino was worn to waxy whiteness
That traced a map of the tiles beneath.

A visitor's cup would have been
One without a chip or two.
A double fold of cardboard
Was thole for a hole in the sole
Of our shoes
Until the wages came through again.

Yet our house was a mecca for many
Who stayed and laughed and played.
Maybe the reason they said
Our home was different,
Was because it was.

They sat long and didn't seem to care
What was going on elsewhere.
Our unmasked ordinariness
Seemed to them
To be pleasingly rare.

A Place at the Table

How many of us think longingly of home when out walking, or shopping, or at work? The key in the lock, the kicking off of shoes, the warmth, the evening meal all promise us rest and relaxation – at least most of the time. For some people however, home is a bit like hospital - with comings and goings, duties of care, endless tasks and responsibilities. Even when night falls and things are hushed outside, the quiet turmoil inside remains. There is little remission in life sometimes.

So where does God find a place in our lives? Is there a time reserved for Him, for prayer, for space that will allow companionship of the most loyal kind? Is there a chair for Him at our fireside, a dinner table place for Him who cares for us with such enduring love? If only those hearts that find themselves near breaking point could stumble instead upon the refuge of His Sacred Heart; a place apart and yet within each soul. If only the isolated and alone could discover the joy of the Gospel, the promises of Christ in the journey! They would find within one greater than themselves. Evangelisation is for the now. The hunger is out there. There is a spiritual famine in the sense that there is bread - but the hungry do not see it, nor their need for it. So swamped are they in the material and secular world that they remain bereft of the treasure of faith.

Love of God

Without the love of God
Where would I be?
I would fear for my soul
And all its longings.

For it is the greatest grace
To hold within my being
The certitude that I am his
And all I love is his
And nothing outside of him matters
Not now
Not tomorrow
Not ever.

Poppies

I stood among the populace of poppies
Long stems spindled delicately
Disc-faces tilted skyward
Drawn to the sun.
And it seemed to me
That the world's greatest allure
Holds nothing more biddable
Before the splendour of God
Than slender poppies
At this morning hour.

The servant of the servants of God moves like the wind, journeys to the back-streets and into the prisons, stands amid the hovels and the squalor of our world and declares the love of a living God. Such actions are as powerful as they are provocative – to us as church, to us as citizens, to you and me.

-

When we look at the figure of Christ upon the Cross we look at every man, rich and poor; for none has lasting wealth unless it was purchased by him, and none is poor that is not made rich in him.

-

Our journey into littleness highlights the greatness of God in a way that invites rather than deters us. We are not trespassers on a great estate but partakers in the sacred mysteries of himself. It is only by becoming small that our minds and hearts can expand enough to take God in. If we pass to him the governance of our hearts, we pass to him our all.

R McD

The local lore tells of a cargo ship that went down
just out beyond the bay.
The following tides gave up from the churning depths
coils of excellent coir.
In the decades since farmers used this odd stuff
to pull breached lambs from birthing ewes;
to tell the circular tale of loss and life,
wreck and rescue.

Strength

Like a tree on the riverbank
Whose branched beauty inclines towards peat-brown
water
My leaning is my strength
I draw upon the goodness
And the warmth
Of a resting place,
Heart-close
Upon the beating breast of God.

Sage

Better to be a cow in the field that knows
The tested friendship of a hawthorn hedge
When wet fists pummel the earth
Than an empire builder
Who has given no time to thinking
Of what he can, and cannot,
Lug over his shoulder
Through blizzards of blinding snow.

At Last

Were I only to accumulate material things
I would retreat into a fog
Of ill-defined borders
Until one day
I might notice
Through a hole the shape of a starfish
In a dimpled glass pane
A thread dangling curiously...

And a sudden compunction might come over me
To reach out beyond myself and pinch that thread
Only to trace its source back to the door of my soul
Where it has been, for ever, seeking entry.

Holy Family

A whistling sound arose from the sea-grasses and rushes
As Joseph walked along the shore
Mary's presence blessed the scene like a prayer
For she was the woman of grace.
And Joseph was strong as the wind
That ruffled the young one's hair.

Bread of Angels

It is faith that leads me into God's garden.
How tiny her hand is!
Small enough to pick the locks
That trap us, stalling our journey towards God.

Hands that can prise open the shell
To reveal the pearl of great price
And hands that can basket
The bread of angels
Entrusted to them at a feast.

Body of Christ

*It is not with glue that God re-sets the broken
fragments of our lives but with himself. He enters
into our brokenness just as he entered into abject
poverty upon a wooden cross. In this world there
are many places and occasions when we hang, as he
did, upon a cross. In our acceptance of it we humble
our unruly hearts and wills and give our very lives
over to the will of God. The mother of the sick child
is at her station and although her body is drained of
energy she knows she will not sleep until her child is
well. She does everything possible to ease the child's
distress and is a source of comfort to the baby. At
the first sign of improvement all tiredness leaves the
mother's body. She could dance round the room
with sheer joy at the sight of her own flesh and
blood regaining colour and strength. Our sins
impoverish us but God died to take our sins away.
We might well thirst for spiritual water like the
man in the bible who waited at the side of the pool.
We can slowly ease ourselves into the healing body
of Christ.*

The Spirit of Light

Calming winds with a simple command
Banishing ills, smoothing to flatness the sands
Raising our minds to heights where holiness dwells
God of all goodness, Lord of the dip and of the swell.

Sower of seed, maker of the stars of night
Will of the Father, Love of the Spirit of light
Fashion our hearts so as to burn with desire
To be moulded to likeness of Him
In the white of the fire.

Greening the pastures with the glance of an eye
Setting in place all under the sky
How great is our God! Amazing in all His ways
Painterly, masterly, potter of earth-bright clays.

Stained Glass
(Reredos at St Patrick's Church, Ringsend, Dublin)

Blueness beckons
And my soul climbs to meet it.
I swim in pools that ease my troubled spirit
And am lost in such a tender rendering
That writes its lover's name
Upon a wall of glass...
And marries in the ceremony of sunlight
This thing of beauty
And this searching soul.

Boats

Oily residue by the water's edge
Has become a feather trap,
A snag for unravelled rope-ends.

They trace out the initials of seafarers long gone
Who drop anchor and swap old yarns,
Talking of currents and cross winds
While skilfully trawling the depths.

Widower

The hands of time deftly eased him
Out of the sodden clothes of mourning.
Freeing his stricken limbs
Like a tree eased from
The cruel bondage of winter
Towards the birthing of new leaves.

Spring romances the world with greenness and
Divulges the secret that it is God himself.
It rises from the well of grief
Into the now of acceptance.

Be holy, for I am holy.

*Good is good, but it is holiness that raises us to a
new level. In striving towards holiness we are
humbling ourselves and acknowledging the source
of all goodness. Our littleness magnifies God's
greatness and our lowliness places us on the altar of
the earth. Our lives then become an ongoing
sacrifice and heart-sourced song of praise.*

'Be holy for I am holy.' Peter 1:16

-

*It might seem that we are losing our way; but we
can come to understand that a good life is a life
given over to the tenderness of God. All things
unfold as they ought, as day follows night.*

-

*Eyes open to God will see God. The first step is a
powerful one because in just one moment we can
move from unbeliever to believer. When our foot
touches down lightly on God's good earth we sense
all about us the embrace of his sweet supporting
love.*

Our Lady of Sorrows

Strangers in the form of sorrows
Darkened Mary's door
One after the other.

Her heart bore piercing wounds
At the cross silently suffering
A living martyrdom
That won for her
A crown of lasting glory.

Rosary Meditation

We may picture Mary as the young mother playing with her child, taking him for walks by the sea, and Joseph crafting a toy boat for Jesus to play with in the shallows. His little hands are barely big enough to hold the wooden vessel yet these hands will one day hold the universal globe while he rests secure in His mother's arms. Icons are windows onto heaven, written and not painted; nothing is added that does not have significance. The mysteries of the rosary assist us in visualising the life and times of the Holy Family of Nazareth. We add ourselves as extra layers to the narrative - to the greatest story ever told. So important are we that the Father knit us together in our mother's womb and God gave us his mother so that we become what Jesus himself was - a son of Mary. And the brotherhood he shares with John is also shared with us as children of the same holy mother. The mysteries of the rosary invite us to contemplate his glorious resurrection as well as his sorrowful passion. We dwell on the joyful mysteries too, and in the mysteries of light we ponder the kingdom and the Eucharist. The rosary helps us look upon Jesus and our world as if through Marian eyes. We can pray that her grace-filled attitude can be ours too and that we in our ordinary lives can, with her assistance, become living icons and walking prayers.

I am what I am in God

I am the tree.
When I am not the tree, I am the field.
When I am not the field I am the breeze
That weaves its way among the leaves.

I am the seed sown.
I am the mound and the hill.
I am the shoal that never sleeps
In a faraway sea where purple weeds are
Rooted in the deep.

I am what I am in God.

Prayer for Souls Searching

Lord may your abiding Word imbue and sanctify souls searching for meaning in life. Grant that beauty will lead all of your children along the way of truth where, with eyes lifted to the hills, we will be ever mindful of each other and our destiny in you.

The Cross

Whether it's polished and gleaming on a plaster wall, or hanging crookedly by a thread in a prison cell, the cross is still the silent witness to our life and the symbol of our salvation. In the silence of the night you might hear its faint song – a kind of dirge, a lament, a keening. If you happen to be awake at dawn you might hear instead a sweet resonance that echoes in the chambers of the heart. Perhaps a strumming on strings, a call to rise to the sweetness of dawn, hints and tinges of light, of hope. This same cross hangs upon the walls of the world and swings in the breeze like a pendulum in the heart, instilling in us a sense of who we are, a purpose....and a sacred knowing.

Lightning Source UK Ltd.
Milton Keynes UK
UKIC02n0201281215
265419UK00001B/10